The Incredible Lives of Monarch Butterflies

Written by Hawys Morgan

Collins

Lots of animals and insects migrate. This means they travel a very long way.

For example, blue whales, turtles and geese migrate across the seas every year.

3

Monarch butterflies also migrate. These incredible butterflies do not weigh very much, but they can make massive trips.

They fly across the skies of North America, over valleys and mountains to Mexico to escape the cold of winter.

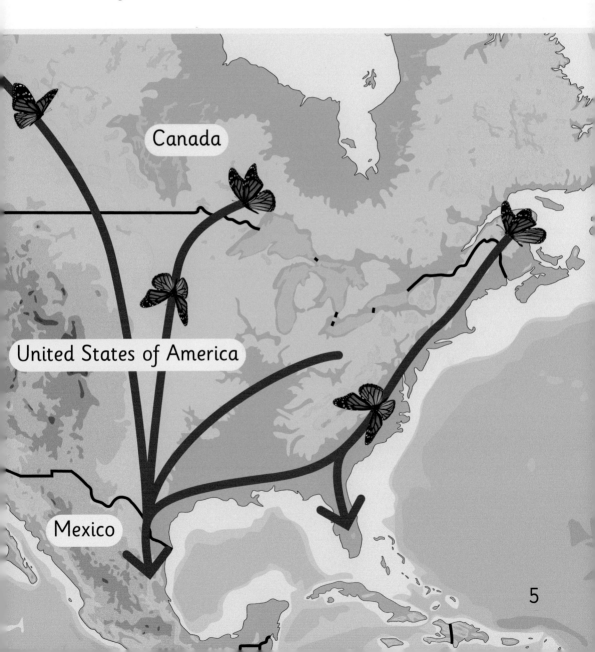

Canada

United States of America

Mexico

Monarch butterflies lay tiny white eggs on milkweed plants.

milkweed plant

They lay an impressive 300 to 500 eggs each.

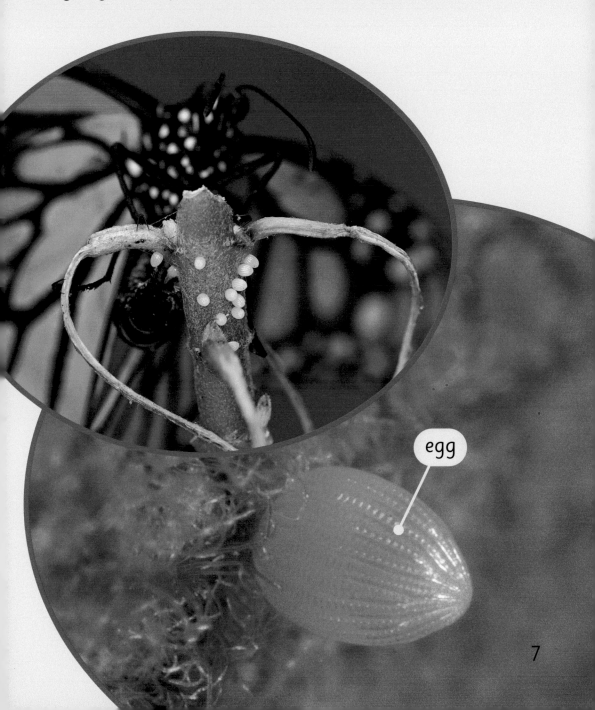

egg

The eggs hatch into brightly striped caterpillars. They rely on a huge supply of milkweed plants to nibble.

It is the only plant they eat. A single greedy caterpillar can munch a leaf in no time!

Once the caterpillar is fully grown, it hangs quietly upside down from a branch.

Over a day, it becomes a fragile chrysalis.
Inside, a butterfly is forming.

chrysalis

After ten days, the chrysalis wobbles. Little by little, the butterfly emerges and stretches its wings.

To begin with, the butterfly's paper-thin wings are crinkled. It twitches them gently to dry them.

As the seasons change, the weather in North America becomes chilly.

So every October, a huge quantity of monarch butterflies leave the chilly north to fly south.

A few months later, they finally arrive in sunny Mexico.

The trip is nearly 3000 km long!

Every year, they fly to the same trees in the mountains.

The butterflies huddle together on the branches.
The tree canopy protects them and keeps them safe.

canopy

After the winter, the butterflies take to the skies. They leave Mexico and head north to find a new supply of milkweed plants.

They lay their eggs on the plants and it all starts again!

Life of a monarch butterfly

caterpillar

chrysalis

butterfly

After reading

Letters and Sounds: Phase 5

Word count: 299

Focus phonemes: /ai/ eigh, a /ee/ e-e, ey, y, e /oo/ u /igh/ ie, y /ch/ tch /c/ ch /j/ g, ge /l/ le /w/ wh /v/ ve /s/ se

Common exception words: of, to, into, the, are, do, once, their

Curriculum links: Science: Animals, including humans

National Curriculum learning objectives: Reading/word reading: apply phonic knowledge and skills as the route to decode words, read other words of more than one syllable that contain taught GPCs; Reading/comprehension: drawing on what they already know or on background information and vocabulary provided by the teacher

Developing fluency

- Your child may enjoy hearing you read the book.
- Take turns to read a page of text, encouraging an enthusiastic tone to emphasise impressive facts.

Phonic practice

- Look together at **chrysalis** on page 11. Challenge your child to separate the syllables as they read the word. (*chrys -al-is*) Check they sound out **ch** as /c/.
- Challenge your child to read these words in the same way too:

  ex-am-ple   in-cred-ib-le   im-press-ive   quan-tit-y   butt-er-fly

Extending vocabulary

- Ask your child to add -y or -ly to each of the words below, to make new words:

  wobble (*wobbly*)   incredible (*incredibly*)

  greed (*greedy*)   crinkle (*crinkly*)

- Can they use these words in a new sentence of their own?